D0728112

good old plastic Jesus

Earnest Larsen, C.SS.R.

Liguorian Books
Liguori, Mo. 63057

photos: Robert Ruhnke, C.SS.R.

art and layout: Gordon Willman

Copyright

Library of Congress Catalog

Card No. 68-8819

Redemptorist Fathers

Liguori, Mo. 63057

Imprimi Potest:

    Raymond Schmitt, C.SS.R.
    Provincial, St. Louis Province
    Redemptorist Fathers

Imprimatur:

    St. Louis, June 21, 1968
    + John J. Carberry
    Archbishop of St. Louis

Art, the young man with the thin beard and quick eyes put it this way, "Life is the constant, pain-filled cry of every living human being to be heard, to be noticed and loved. Joy is the rare moment when the cry breaks through and someone momentarily hears it. Joy is being heard — on a deeper level — being the one who hears."

Downstairs in the tiny, tattered Mennonite Church another member of the in-service-workers was teaching a local youth group Christmas songs of peace, brotherhood and a man named Christ.

Joy is lightning that leaps between the temples of men's souls. When the flash is spent there is no doubt but that God has made his presence felt among men . . . The lightning doesn't depend on who the men are; it depends on the condition of their souls.

(GOD'S BEAUTIFUL ONES,
by Julian Kern Rody)

7

4:30

afternoon in a

HUGE!CLANG
ING!!RUSHIN
G!!!CITY

A prophet stands on a corner
in the middle of it all —
watching.
Not a prophet with a beard,
threatening,
dressed in rough clothes,
calling down vengeance —
but someone who sees,
who understands,
who listens,
who is one with the life around him.

The million-eyed office buildings
open,
people pour out,
quitting time.
Cars honking
crowding
speeding between blocks.

red light

brakes squeal

green light

screech off again.
Executives in a hurry
"Give me a Scotch" —
little old ladies
everywhere
shopping bags bulging
curious to see everything.
The cats parade by, tough guys
shades
fancy hats
action.

"City … I own you"

Police direct traffic

keep things going!
don't let them JAM!
GET GOING over there.

School girls troop by
brown and yellow uniforms
talking about volleyball championship.
Radiating

life!

too much for anyone to hold.
The prophet watches
taking it all in —

school girls
winos
millionaires
paperboys sixty years old;
the city in motion
everyone running
hurrying
to pay homage to their God
whoever and whatever he is.
Burning incense before the shrine.

Suddenly in the prophet's eyes
everything begins to fade away
everything becomes so clear —
what is REALLY happening all around him.
The city stands before God
each person offering what he is
or thinks he has of value.
It's important,
everyone
must offer Something.
They all watch each other
sometimes jealous
sometimes approving
sometimes mocking.
A loud pushy man bulls his way up
proudly
confidently.
Shouts at God,
"I'll tell you what I offer:
shrewd business
clever bargains
smart deals
money.
You sent me out ignorant
but look how much I made of myself;
see how wise I am now!"
Everyone cheers
applauds.
"What a fabulous thing to offer God."
"He's a cool operator"
"Man, he's got it made."

MONEY

Next
A young man walks forward
stands before God
before the people.
Unimpressed,
cocky,
yet, he hesitates.
The City is bored.
"He's just a kid."
"Hope he doesn't take too long."
"He doesn't have anything to offer anyway."
"Hey, you, hurry up!"
The young man looks around slowly
at all the people
at God.
"God,
what do I have to offer?
That man had a smart life;
maybe it pleased you;
I'm not sure."

15

The City broke in —
"Hurry up!"
"There's a lot of us waiting."
"We have important things."
"God doesn't have all day to waste."
The young man just stands there.
Then his face starts to glow,
to burn.
An idea, a realization,
sets his soul on fire,
"God, I offer you Me.
Right now — youth,
the thrill
of a car leaping forward,
speed on a dark highway.
Energy
bursting energy
at the discovery of an idea,
the difference an ideal makes.
You know,
the difference — it matters.
I offer you the agony
frustration
rage
of living with so many
who don't understand.
It's so

simple!

but they just don't understand.

These hands
these feet
these eyes
ache to discover
to find music to dance to
to live to.
They are ALIVE
NOT dead, Living.
My mind
imagination
memory
are yours.
Sure, a million times a million mistakes
will roll from them;
ideas come and go like snow,
falling snow.
A million more will come, before old age
like winter
moves in and freezes them.
Yours is the questioning
dissatisfaction.
Success.
Failure.
ME."

The people again mumble,
"He's crazy!"
"Making a big deal of nothing."
"Who does he think he is?"
"God will laugh at him, or get mad!"
The young man
cared less
what they thought of his gift.
He throws his arms wide open;
"I offer you a body that wants to dance
and sometime die
for something worthwhile,
I know there **IS**
something worthwhile.
A mouth to sing
or shout about injustice
or cry if it gets hurt too badly.
I offer you time.

NOW!

a countless number of thrills
yet to come.
I offer you my **firsts:**
the **first** understanding of what a friend is,
knowing that I have one,
that someone
honestly
sincerely
cares
about me,
and I them.

The first discovery of love,
the agony of
'You'll get over it; it's just puppy love.'
Maybe so,
but right now it's ME.
I want to GET OUT
and go
and go
and go.
Meet new people,
do new things.
I'm tired of sitting around
doing the same things
ALL the time.
I want to get OUT
of Myself
get rid of all my stupid fears
and SAY something,
a word,
something **important** to someone.

If this sounds funny...
stupid... I'm sorry
but, I don't apologize for it,
I offer it to you.

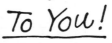
To You!

Not what I have done,
the sharp deals, but what
I am and want _to be_
and _will_ do. I offer
you this tremendous
longing.

At times for things without names.
But they must be;
I feel them deep inside.
God, I offer you the present
and the future
and my flight into it."
He stood there happy
proud.
The people of the City were indignant,
"He's crazy."
"Finally he quit."
"Let God get a word in edgewise."
"He'll hear about taking up all that time now."
God quietly looked at all the people.
For a long time he held the young man
with his young, million-year-old eyes.
"Greater love
no man has given ME.
The Precious Gift, himself."
God looked full into the young man's face
and eyes
and heart.
A rain of fire swept into his soul.
All at once,
suddenly,
FINALLY
he was able to grab hold —
to understand —
the true meaning of all the fine words
so often spoken
so often empty.
He felt like exploding.

"You will find that which has no name"
said God.
"It is my name,

I AM WHAT YOUR BURSTIN

My love for you
has no bounds.
No word can hold it,
except my Word,
the Word of God,
Whom I have spoken to you."
The people were amazed.
"Do you think he's kidding?" some whispered.
"See how God is looking at that kid,
It's no joke, It's for real."

The court began to fade away
in the prophet's eyes.
The buses bullied their way along.
Cars screeched and darted,
people hurried along.
To where?
To do what?

TOWARD!

PLASTIC JESUS

"He (Jesus Ortiz) crossed himself as he kneeled, then got to his feet and passed all the saints until he got to the altar where the crucified figure hung patiently in the dimness. He kneeled again at the low rail and rested his chin on his arms to stare. . . . He smiled faintly. . . . It was a fairy tale; he wondered why he had allowed himself obeisance to it. Santa Claus hadn't survived his fourth year. Still, it was quiet here; the candles and the faint smell of incense eased his restlessness. Would he have dared to come if he believed? . . . The blood hung in the wooden wounds. And a white Jesus Christ at that! 'Oh man, you don't know the half of it,' he said silently to the statue above him; 'it's too complicated for you.' . . . Why the hell had he come here? Why did he stay? Oh, who knows? Just . . . there times when you completely alone by yourself and nothin' in this world make sense. It was quiet here . . . he could rest a little, even on his knees, with his head on his hands. That man up on the cross weren't gonna do him no harm, at least that for sure." (THE PAWNBROKER, by Edward Lewis Wallant)

Today

is for Searching —
for anxiously trying on new ideas.
It gets frustrating!

So much turns out to be BUBBLES,

flimsy illusions that break
leaving us emptyhanded.

eXPeRTS
are a
DIME a
DOZEN

they can tell you
the INS and
OUTS of

EVERYTHING.

what is

FOR SURE!

And it still doesn't quite make sense.
At times (maybe often) one of those things is

GOD.

It's easy to think in our hearts
but not out loud — (**"Of course** you believe!)
". . . Oh God, you don't know the half of it . . . ."
The question though —
isn't God or Not God
but
H O W to make Him REAL.
So often He just doesn't seem to be around.
Not really.

Often he is the "Plastic Jesus"
Paul Newman sang about in COOL HAND LUKE.
". . . I don't care if it rains or freezes.
As long as I got my Plastic Jesus,
Everything will be fine."
But even Luke said,

"There's been a failure to communicate here."

We are supposed to find God through
Church
prayers
sacraments
statues.
But sometimes NONE of these
comes across.
And we feel like screaming,
"GOD — please,
I want Y O U.
I need you,
not just laws and dogmas about you.
I need you.

someone!

some ONE!

Someone who will walk with me
trust me
challenge me. Through all the confusion,
all the mistakes,
a With-Me-God.
And REALLY,
really, I know you ARE
a someONE.
Someone who will not let me compromise
be satisfied
with being
mediocre.
A someONE who loves me enough
to push me
drag me above
the pettiness of this world
to be a someONE too, a
someone worthwhile — doing worthwhile
things."

the living God
is a person.

Plastic Jesus is a

thing

We can search for God
as a PERSON or a thing.
If we want a person and reach
for a thing
we will get a thing
that can never be a person.

When
God, Church, Sacraments, Liturgy become
things — forget God.
He isn't there.

When God becomes a person who loves **us**
and asks for a like response
BECAUSE He loves us
then
Religion is real.
The Church
becomes the spirit of man
struggling to become ONE.
The sacraments become rain sinking into the earth:
God-With-Man.
Liturgy becomes the hymn of all living men
swelling together from the four corners of the earth
through the one Priest, Christ
to the Father,
that we may have LIFE
and have it more abundantly.
If the Sacraments — Liturgy — are "things we do"
we lose.
We DO things
we LIVE
with a
Person we love.

Prayer — is NOT
"a time for saying words."
It's simply the overflow of a heart that
KNOWS it is always
in the presence
— a communicating presence —
of a trusted,
loved SOMEONE.
Sometimes the overflow is
spoken
sometimes not;
sometimes formal
sometimes just soul talk;

sometimes alone, (maybe walking in the rain — or
waiting for a light to change
or doing dishes
or going downstairs to breakfast)
sometimes in common-unity with many others.
But **ALWAYS**
just the overflow of a person who has said
YES
to someone.
Without that —

zero
0000000000

hello
plastic
jesus

by-laws and procedure of

religion business

1 The boss is God.
He owns the company.
It you're going to get
anywhere, be a yes man,
play ball — it's smart.

2 The purpose is to buy shares
in the Company. To buy
you go
through certain motions — keep
certain laws. You don't have to
really MEAN them, just do them.
Punch into church
like a timeclock —
it insures good standing.

3

Play the game and you get paid.
The pay is grace. Build up a big
bank roll. The Boss, God, keeps
close tabs on your account.
When the business deal is over
He checks out the books, if you
have enough in the old grace-roll you
get a cool place called heaven.
(At least everyone says it's cool.)

4

Purpose of the whole affair —
to keep enough grace socked away
so that in case the game comes to
a sudden end
you don't come out a loser.
And the Boss is pretty strict
about the whole thing.

smart business

miserable religion

In fact it isn't "religion."
No one buys religion
by doing things.
There is no
snappy reward for doing things.
No spiritual merit badge.
Religion is a re-union
a coming together
a living with.
A meeting and seeing God
as a Person
Who accepts us
for what we ARE.
Loves us
for what we ARE.
Invites us to friendship,
SONSHIP
with HIM.

If —
if we take this invitation from God
seriously,
accepting what He told us about himself
as a Person,
then a lot of things look different.
God
is not just the directing
ruling
law-giver from
"heaven above,"
but MEANING
entering our lives in a billion ways
answering the needs of our heart.
So very visible,
touchable in the infinity
man finds in his own heart
after he pushes the real important questions
as far as he can —
and still there is no answer.
There is only
the ability to go further,
the
ENDLESS capacity to know more
feel more
become more.

god

He is more than spiritual aspirin
to cure our **now-here**
now-gone problems.
More than an indifferent string puller
whom we can blame
for the world's tears.
Find God
and we will know who looks back at us
from the deepest mirror
of our own heart.

What does it mean to open to God
as a Person,
to let Him live
as a Person,
to come down from the metal dash boards,
out of the plastic statues?

To really meet God
or anyone,
an open mind is a must.

A
CLOSED MIND
IS
A CLOSED
HEART.

"Sure,

I know

what
Negroes, Puerto Ricans, kids with long hair,
rich people, poor people,
middle-class people, artists,
intellectuals are like. I don't have
to meet any; I just know."
To know
"what they're like" eliminates discovering
WHO they are;
eliminates the possibility
of being friends.

The high school football hero
wants to DO
something "NICE."
Someone suggests,
"Go down to the inner city
and be a big brother to some
of THEM."
"Forget it!
I know what they're like.
Bad News."

But, finally
he goes.
Goes to "help **them.**"
He flops
Miserably . . .
trying to Do things before
he becomes someONE.
Slowly, his blindness leaves him.
He begins to see people.
Finds kids who are just kids —
not things —
kids looking for the same friendship,
acceptance
security
the same joy as any kid.
They aren't
"Them"
anymore.
He isn't
a **tin** god
anymore,
"saving unfortunates — ."

Now
he shares with the people
grows with them.
He gains
MORE
than the kids
ever dreamed of. . .

An open heart
is an open mind.

delinquents?

delinquents? sure I know what they're like..... _cheap!_

A woman visits
her friend,
a delinquent
in a reform school.
She talks to her
like a "her,"
not an "it."
The "delinquent"
(the cheap girl)
is playing her guitar,
singing
her own songs
about
being loved
caring for someone
being important to someone —
anyone.
Without her mask,
just her —

BEAUTIFUL.
Softness deeply glowing,
free of the bitter hiding.

Two minutes later
the ward mother storms in.
"Put that away."
"It's study time."
"Always pulling something."
"You problem kids are all alike."
Up goes the mask
tough,
cheap,
mean.

WHICH
IS
WORSE?
BLIND
EYES

OR
BLIND

HEARTS?
"SURE I

WHAT
DELINQUENTS

ARE

LIKE"

And God — well certainly we know what He
is like.
All Powerful
ruler
leader —
God of long ago who spoke on a
mountain somewhere.
Oh?

God
revealed himself through HIS
mirror,
Jesus Christ.
"Once there was a Father . . ."
" . . . I AM the good Shepherd . . ."
" . . . You are no longer servants, but friends . . ."
" . . . We will come to you
and make our abode with YOU."
CRUCIFIED,
to create a sun for the world.
RISEN
to make the sun rise for the world
of MEN.
A Million lives of constant meditation
would
NEVER
scratch the surface of WHO
God IS.
" . . . the Way
the Truth,
Life."

The meaning behind all meaning
the beauty behind all beauty
the steel of men's courage
the endless mystery and wonder of all things.
IMPOSSIBLE
for any
living man to say,
"I know it all — what else is there to prove?"
We Prove **things**.
We undertake an endless journey of discovery with
people we
love.
"I know all that stuff
they teach about God"
might be true
of "that stuff"
but not of God.

We can make it tough for God
to speak to us.

hey boy! what can you do?

100% way to destroy
any possibility
of meeting
anyone.

"I don't care who you are —
what can you do?
Can you be of
U S E
to me? If so,
hang around."
We can know a lot ABOUT
someone and never
know that person at all.

A girl can be a great
cheerleader
guitar player
horsewoman
artist
but who is SHE?

A boy can be a fantastic
football player
car mechanic
chess player
dancer.
Who is
He?
"Who are they?"
CANNOT
be answered by
"what can they do?"
"God,
Mr. Fix-it,
Complaint department deluxe,
court of highest appeals —
God,
you can wipe out the slums
stop the war
make everything easy.
Step in.
Do it."
Christ made
the blind see
the lame walk
the mute speak
the dead live again.
BUT
miracles are picture frames.
LOOK;
Who is IN the frame?

Who
IS
God?
"Hey God,
what can You do?
Are you useful?"
Ask
the wrong question
we'll get
the wrong answer.

GOD IS

the farmer sowing his seed of vision
the fisherman casting his nets of reality
the madman of Calvary
scorning phoniness to Blood
the victorious conqueror of isolation and death.

HE IS

the never-ending horizon of infinite friendship
we journey into —
through the port
of each man we meet.
God who IS
doesn't answer the mealy
drab
attitude
"What can you do?"

And He is not in the attitude:
classify,
catalogue,
categorize,
divide, store, sort out.

KILL

"Finally, I got you figured."
"I have your number."
"Now I got you pegged."
"I know what you're gonna say
before you open your mouth."
"Ask me a question — I have an answer."
All attitudes that fit THINGS
not people
not love
Not God.
Love is discovery
without end.
When the searching dies
the love dies.
But God, —
"Figure Him out"
"Gather Him inside our walls"
"Understand all about Him."

How easy to say
"I do not understand why this happened to me!
God must not BE."
Job —
remember Job?
He finally got fed up with God.
Things didn't
work out.

God did.

"Friend, where were you
when I founded the earth?
Have you ever entered
the sources of the sea?
Have you ever walked about
behind death's door?

Tell Me if you know all; which is the way
to the dwelling place of the light —
where is the home of the night?"
Will the critic argue with God? Then let him
who would correct God give some answers.

We are luckier than Job.
We are Christ-born,
New Covenant.
We know more about God through Christ,
more about ourselves,
about the way things **Really** are.
We know more about
man's freedom,
God's love for us.
There is a saying, "To complain
to God is to worship."
But,
there is all the difference
in the world between complaining
to a Person
who loves us
and to
a Mr. Fix-IT.
The Loving Person will answer,
as He did to Job.
Mr. Fix-it is
deaf
dumb
blind
nowhere.
Mr. Fix-It fits into a neat category.
God doesn't,

many friendships
never come to be...

because one or both is afraid
to take a chance,
to RISK.
"I'll be your friend
IF
it doesn't cost too much."
Can't happen.
To accept friends
is to accept their
good points — bad points —
strengths — weaknesses —
wonderful traits — wacky foibles.
Take them for whatever
may come in the future.
Their joys
are our joys;
their sorrows —
"Share them with me."
Anyone not willing to pay
the price of friendship
is Not
worthy of it.
(And will never find it.)

God challenges.
Those not willing to accept this challenge
don't really want a living God.
For them
Plastic Jesus is fine.
He doesn't ask anything.
He's easy.
Approach God
OPENLY
sensitive to what He
IS
aware of His infinite mystery
and He will challenge **you**.
The challenge:
BE TRUE TO YOURSELF.
COME ALIVE
to everything in the world that is.
The challenge of God is the risk of
openness.
Meet God along the path of life as a
Person
a friend,
and He will be a life-long companion.
But you
will have to walk where
He walks.
Where is He not present?
Where does he not live and die,
rise and fall,
rejoice and despair?

God does not offer a bed of roses.
He offers a world with ups and downs, but
a world in progress.
He will set us in a thousand
desperate places,
places where we are needed,
and ask us to be true.
He
will not baby us,
shield us **from**
pain
He will lead us **through**
pain
loneliness,
frustration
searching
to the strong gentle wisdom
He alone can create in us.
We will meet countless starving
PEOPLE,
starving for kindness
for acceptance.
STARVING
for someONE
to take them as they are,
starving for the confidence to
overcome mistrust of themselves
of others
of everything.

Confidence we give — **if**
we will have confidence in them.
God's challenge:
BE TRUE
TO ME
by being true
to yourself.

will you feed my sheep?

His way may well not lead us to foreign
places
or — the inner city,
or Vista
or Peace Corps
or Extension
but to such needy places as our own home,
our own family.
He will take us to such difficult
places as our own
school
and corridors
and classrooms,
to the one next to us in study hall.
(Even THEM!)
Those whom we may have never seen
but need our friendship
as we need theirs.
God is NOT for
FREE.
Neither is the exquisite
JOY
of being alive,
for they are the same.
Plastic Jesus is free — he is easy.
But the meaning of God's name is the
meaning
of His challenge,
to **Become**
a **SomeONE.**

The most
important door
to God
is named

freedom

A million
years
of force
is not enough
to "have God"
One second
of free
humble
accepting
is enough
for a lifetime.
And then some.
Imagine
someone saying
"You
HAVE to be
my friend,
you have to."
Forget it.

In a tiny restaurant of
North Chicago, a
friendship grew.
Terell, an inner city teenager, and
Mr. Maurice, a college professor,
often stopped at Ben's
for hamburgers.
Complete strangers,
Terell:
goatee
Black T-shirt
ankle weights (football was coming up)
dark shades.
Mr. Maurice:
smooth
white shirt
classy tie
brief case (full of complicated papers)
conservative suit.
No one said they HAD to be friends.
Terell was there on
a government-sponsored program
but there are no
government-sponsored friendships.
It began spontaneously,
naturally grew.
Grew strong.
At first,
"Pass the ketchup."
"This seat taken?"
"Gimme the cream."
Then
"How's school?"

"Where do you live?"
"College teaching must be weird."
Met more — talked more
Talked more — learned more
Learned more — accepted more
All the rules of friendship were there —

especially FREEDOM

A free choice FOR
God?
Not to make a decision
against God
is NOT
to make a positive choice
for Him.
Easy to float.
Mass: "I gotta go."
Confession: "Who wants to go to hell?"
Liturgy: "My mom is on my back."

free choice?

Many times we think we HAVE
to love God.
Look at all He's done for us.
Besides,
we are supposed to;
almost everyone says so.
After all, He IS
God . . .
No one
HAS
to love God
or anyone.
We can't "have to."
No one can draw a round circle.
If we will love God
go to Him on a
level of
Faith.
It must be by freely accepting
the invitation He first freely held out.
No other way will work,
EVER.
God — coming through to us as open
and loving,
ready to take a risk
willing to reveal himself as Person.
We — responding in kind.
Then everything starts to make sense.
especially
FAITH.

3.

FAITH IS
SOMETHING
ELSE

To be free, to be able to stand
up & leave everything
behind ... without looking
back. To say, Yes!

dag hammarskjold / markings

To talk about faith
at best
is elusive.
Like God, it too, is not
"a thing,"
but the basic thread woven into the combination
steel armor
and wedding garmet
that is LIFE.
Yet when it takes root
in a man
there is no mistake
that it is present.
Faith gives a vision
a goal
an unshakable conviction
which gives life deep meaning.
Not necessarily
answers —
but meaning, purpose, reason.
The greatest pauper is the "no-where man"
stumbling around
devoid of any faith.
Faith is Freedom.
Hammarskjold simply spells it
"YES."
A complete, wholehearted **Y E S**.
Not to simple facts
or intellectual theories —
no matter how interesting they may be —

but a YES to a CODE
a vision of life that
could be,
that MUST be;
a code first given and lived
by a man who had the ability
to enflame others with his
belief.
Christ,
Mohammed,
Napoleon,
Lenin,
Kennedy:
all had the ability
to inspire a YES
from their followers.

This is freedom —
the **only** freedom from the apathetic
dog-eat-dog
"so what"
world of status-seeking today.
Faith is the commitment to a better way.

Christian Faith is more.
It is a gift that first
must be given.
Christ is more than man.
His message is
the WORD.
The flowering,
the fulfillment
of every truth the prophets of
religion
politics
social awareness
have confronted ordinary man with
when he was in danger
of pulling down his own house.

Christ —
the Word of God.
The Word that liberates,
that

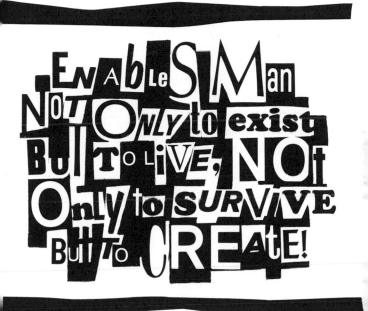

ENABLES MAN NOT ONLY to exist BUT TO LIVE, NOt Only to SURVIVE BUt TO CREATE!

Faith lives.
Its code never takes the easy way
OUT.
To say

YES!

is to be prepared to stand up —
and not look back.

General McArthur knew about faith.
He put it into three words
and spoke about these words in his last
farewell to his beloved West Point:

duty - honor - country

those words ... dictate what you ought to be ... can be
... will be. They are your rallying points: to build
courage when courage seems to fail; to rebuild faith
when there seems to be little cause for faith; to create
hope when hope becomes forlorn. ...

They build character ... make you strong enough to
know when you are weak ... brave enough to face
yourself when you are afraid ... to be proud and un-
bending in honest failure ... humble and gentle in
success ... not to substitute words for action, nor seek
the path of comfort, but to face the spur and stress of
difficulty and challenge; to learn to stand up in the
storm but have compassion on those who fall; to
master yourself before you seek to master others; to
have a heart that is clean, a goal that is high; to learn
to laugh yet never forget how to weep; to reach into
the future yet never neglect the past; to be serious yet
never to take yourself too seriously.

In my memory's eye I could see those staggering columns of the First World War, bending under soggy packs ... from dripping dusk to drizzling dawn, slogging ankle deep through the mire of shell-shocked roads, to form grimly for the attack, blue-lipped, covered with sludge and mud, chilled by the wind and rain; driving home to their objective and for many, to the judgment seat of God ...

Always for them — Duty — Honor — Country; always their blood, sweat and tears as we sought the way and the light and the truth. And twenty years later, on the other side of the globe, again the filth of murky foxholes ... boiling suns ... devastating storms; the loneliness and utter desolation ... the vision of gaunt, ghastly men reverently following your password of Duty — Honor — Country. . . .

The Long Gray Line has never failed us. Were you to do so, a million ghosts in olive drab, in brown khaki, in blue and gray would rise from their white crosses thundering those magic words — Duty — Honor — Country.

Faith is a code that sets men free.
Not free to talk about it,
think about it,
argue about it —
but WORTHY to LIVE it.

Religion, faith, differs greatly
from "just" a subject learned
in school
like any other.
Faith is something else.
It is not a shrinking flower
protectively hoarded
by old women,
but a tempest
capable of turning men's hearts to fire.
A tremendous shout of joy,
a mission to re-create this world
into something MORE —
to make man
MORE than flesh and blood.
Faith fails
NOT
because it is weak,
but because there are not enough men and women
open enough
to hear its challenge,
brave enough
to say YES,
big enough
to love

till their cup runs over

SURE, I BELIEVE!

Lots of people say that.
Lots of people think faith is just answering affirmative
to questions.

Teacher:
"Do you believe Jesus Christ is God?"

Elmo:
"Yes."

Teacher:
"Do you believe He became man?"

Elmo:
"Sure."

Teacher:
"Do you
believe He died,
rose from the dead,
instituted a Church and through baptism you
become **part** of that Church?"

Elmo:
"Sure enough."

Teacher:
"Do you **really** believe Jesus Christ is present
in the Blessed Sacrament?"

Elmo:
"Of course."
Teacher:
"Do you believe your sins are forgiven
in confession?"
Elmo:
"They'd better be,
after all the times I went."

Lots of nice affirmative answers.
Does it of itself mean faith is there?
Not at all.
"Sure,
I believe;
ask me any question."
Faith doesn't work that way.
People didn't just
believe
what
Kennedy said;
they believed
IN him.
Kennedy the man.
They said,
LEAD.
We're right behind YOU.
This is the kind of faith
Christ asks
and deserves
from us.

Like the blind man
Christ nearly passed up,
"Jesus, Son of David, have mercy."
"Hey, quiet, you're making too much noise,"
said the crowd.
What did he care?
It was Jesus — all the louder,
"Son of David have mercy!"

Or
the woman who washed His feet
"...it He only knew what kind of a woman..."
She could care less what the Pharisees
thought of her.
Jesus was here, that's enough.
Faith
is that kind of reality.

A lot of people
say
they've lost their faith;
but many never had it at all.
You can't lose
real faith like a
five dollar bill
or ball game
or pair of glasses.
Those are things.
Faith is LIFE.
When it's gone you **know**
a terribly important
deep source of meaning
is gone.
Plastic Jesus is easy
to get rid of.
Not God.

where does
faith start?
how does
it grow?
what's it
made of?

"In the Beginning"
is REVELATION.
Just a fancy word.
It means, I step from behind
my
walls
my
masks
and say: "This is ME,
what I really am
how I really think
how I really feel."
People can bum around together
a long time
at school
at work
in the neighborhood
and never talk, not really.
If they ever do,
revelation happens.
They find they are pretty much
alike —
same fears
same wants
same hopes
same gripes;
and they know each other
differently
more deeply
more truly.

But any revelation
if
It is to lead
ANYWHERE
demands an answer:
Faith.
Reject the revelation of another person,
"Phoney"
"I don't believe it,"
"Who cares?"
"Stop bothering me,"
AND IT DIES.
Faith says,
"I believe in YOU."
Not just things you say —
facts
statistics —
But **YOU.**
Dave and Judy are happily married.
Their love
so gently strong.
Sometimes Judy tries so hard to
SAY things.
But the words jam up.
She gets tongue-tied
gum-balled
embarrassed.
Dave touches her shoulder.
Nothing else is needed.
It's okay.
She is Judy.
He is Dave;
they accepted each other.
They believe.
This is Faith.

revealed himself IN and THROUGH
Jesus Christ.
Speaking to man,
the Word.
In a thousand ways —
through
liturgy
scripture
sacraments
people around us
the world in which we live.
He speaks
and speaks
and speaks,
trying to break through our deafness,
"THIS IS ME."
"I THIRST FOR YOU."
To reject the free revelation —
sterility.
God takes us seriously
as we are — persons.
Our response,
IF
it is the same,
spells love — communication.
If
it is not,
it spells plastic.

a blind
eye sees
no
light; a
deaf
ear hears
no
Music

An attitude of borodom
OR FORCED PRESENCE
or taking a person for granted,
reduces that person to a thing.
Communication — IMPOSSIBLE.

A marriage taken for granted
is a stone tragedy.
No searching
no wonder
no awe
there is little revelation.
("why bother?")
So, no free acceptance in faith of the other.
The couple no longer consider it
an honor,
a privilege,
to love THIS man,
THIS woman.

God's revelation is free,
free because he is LOVE.
To take Him for granted — uninterested —
("God — so what!")
tunes **us** OUT.
Not God.
God does not ask for
or want
a forced, cold reverence —
fear:
"Don't whisper in church."
"Keep your head covered."
"Use the holy water."
This is plenty for Plastic Jesus.

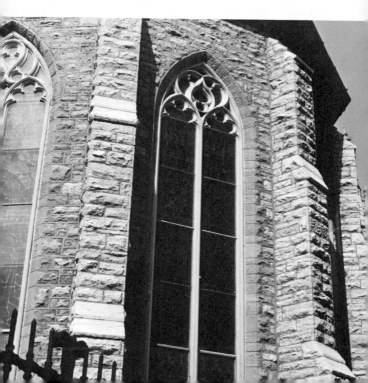

God
seeks an openhearted, joyous
Yes
to life
with all its ups and downs.
This God WHO loves the little children,
who spoke of feasts,
flowers growing in the fields,
farmers who work the land,
fishermen who fish the sea,
"YES!
COME TO ME."
To come,
whether in liturgy or in quiet moments
with an attitude of boredom
with no idea of REALLY communicating with
a PERSON
makes finding Him
impossible.
An open heart
that knows GOD IS,
that comes alive to the challenge,
the VISION
of mankind re-created
and his part with it
begins a journey into God
that will never end.

People communicate
through signs.
There is no other way.
Signs spanning two people
are bridges
over which meaning travels.
But people make signs.
Between poor senders
and poor receivers
are poor signs
and little communication.

Words are signs,
and gifts,
letters,
and flowers.
A prom corsage
pressed in a scrapbook
speaks volumes.

People make signs.
A goofy valentine
between friends
is beautiful.
A tiny smile,
a gesture
between two people who understand,
who share a secret,
speak more than any words.

A sign is a sign when it is seen with the heart.
A wedding ring is a sign —
on newlyweds the bands of metal
are not metal,
but two lives eternally united.
On a tray in a pawnshop
they mean
nothing.
There they are only
metal
and remain just
metal.
A sign not accepted with the heart
is no sign.

A dog can leave a biscuit for another dog;
it only means
he is no longer hungry.
Never
"I love you."
A starving man says just
that
in leaving food for another.

A girl receives candy from a boy.
She says,
"Good, I'm hungry; besides,
I like this kind."
He was saying, "you are special."
One spoke with the heart;
one just with the eyes.
There's been a failure to
communicate here.

Signs don't just
happen.
People make signs.
God's signs are **everywhere**.
Good receivers
are not.

GOD
signs to man
HE
signed so hard the Sign
took flesh + Blood
lived for us
died
+ rose

so we might join Him,
shout Yes to Him
create with Him.
God's sign was a Word,
the Word of God,
Jesus.

But any sign,
even Jesus,
if not seen with heart
is mute
plastic.
Another name for sign,
for Jesus,
is Sacrament.
A sacrament is
not "a thing to do,"
but a bridge upon which
people
meet God,
communicate,
understand,
and become ONE.
Sacrament —
Jesus —
is NOT in competition with,
NOT separated from
the deeply human signs
like wedding rings
fraternity pins
letter sweaters
flowers saved.

Sacraments enrich everything truly human.
They are communications:
God-With-Us;
we, more like God.
People
vastly more capable
of loving
of creating;
not weak —
   running at the first refusal of acceptance or
   backing off
   because true love costs plenty —
but strong —
  responding to Gods challenge —
BECOME.
We can destroy ANY sign:
"Why do I HAVE to go to church?"
"How far can I go?"
"I hate to get involved."
"Will God send me to hell?"
"Church takes too long!"
God
signed so hard
the Sign took flesh
and bled —
"Hear Me."
But a sign
is no sign
if not seen with the heart.

No one just **"HAS"** faith.
To have it is to live it.
Faith grows
develops
matures
as we do.
Like maturity it is
NEVER reached
but reached for.
Faith is not HAD
automatically
at baptism
or graduation.

As long as we can grow as persons,
faith can grow more genuine.
Situations in life change.
Relationships change.
So must faith.
If faith doesn't grow, it atrophies.
Childhood faith is not enough
for teenage;
teenage faith is not enough
for adulthood.
Children want dependence
protection,
poetry;
their faith must include this.
Teenage faith is something else.
It is a time to break away
to identify
to search for answers.
Faith
is not outside of this.
It is part of it.

To question
does not mean
DEAD faith.
Dead people do not search
or question
or wonder;
they do not crave to
understand
or feel
or experience.

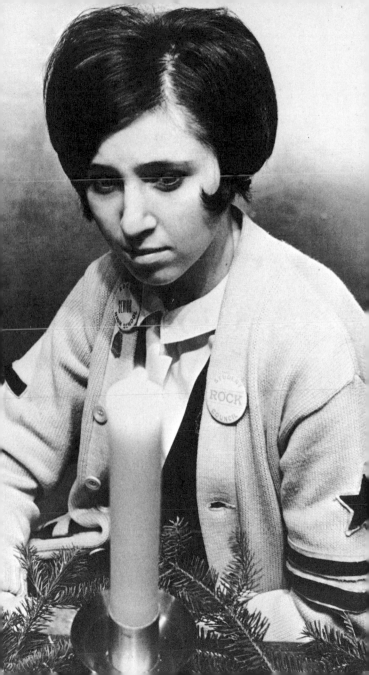

A girl said,
"I do not believe.
I want to feel God too much.
What color is His skin?
What is the sound of His voice?
The meaning of His name?"
She does not believe,
in **Plastic Jesus**
or the Church as simply
a building of stone
or mere facts **about** someone
in place of a **living** oneness
with someone.
But she believes
in God.

Another,
"I'm too alive to believe.
I love dancing,
sports,
games
picnics
parties.
I feel deeply
with the people of Vietnam,
the social agonies of our time.
Just too alive."

But Faith

IS

being alive;
alive to
the world
accepting
your responsibility
in the world,
as someone
who has a
Word
to speak.

"Yes, we shall set them (Christians) to work, but in their leisure hours we shall make their life like a child's game, with children's songs and innocent dance. Oh, we shall allow them even sin, they are weak and helpless, and they will love us like children because we allow them to sin . . . And we shall take it upon ourselves, and they will adore us as their saviors who have taken on themselves their sins before God . . . We shall have an answer for all. And they will be glad to believe our answer, for it will save them from the great anxiety and terrible agony they endure at present in making a free decision for themselves." (THE BROTHERS KARAMAZOV, by Fedor Dostoyevsky)

YOU BET!
THIS IS ME!

Dostoyevsky loved Christ,
detested
the Catholic Church.
In his book Christ returns
freeing
urging
elevating
preaching the word,
the good news.
The Church imprisons Him
puts him on trial.
The charge:
You didn't REALLY love
man;
you set him free,
free to decide
free to live
  or die
Free to choose slavery
  or liberty
Free to accept his own
dignity
value
worth
  or reject it.
See —
You didn't love man at all.
"Man is not strong enough to bear freedom.
We
have loved man.
we
have taken away his responsibility;

it is so much easier that way;
We'll decide for him."
Dostoyevsky had a lame idea
of the Church,
but not of freedom.
Without responsibility
there is no freedom.
We can be
either
good
or bad;
either
sinful
or loving.
These are all choices.
Choices must be free.
No person
thing
institution
can carry the responsibility for us.
Anyone
not ready
to bear the great anxiety,
terrible agony,
of making his own decisions
will not be free —
is not worthy to be free.
Dostoyevsky thought most men
were not strong enough.
Often
history has proved him correct.

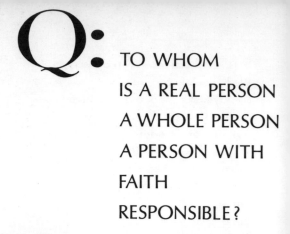

Q: TO WHOM
IS A REAL PERSON
A WHOLE PERSON
A PERSON WITH
FAITH
RESPONSIBLE?

A: TO HIMSELF

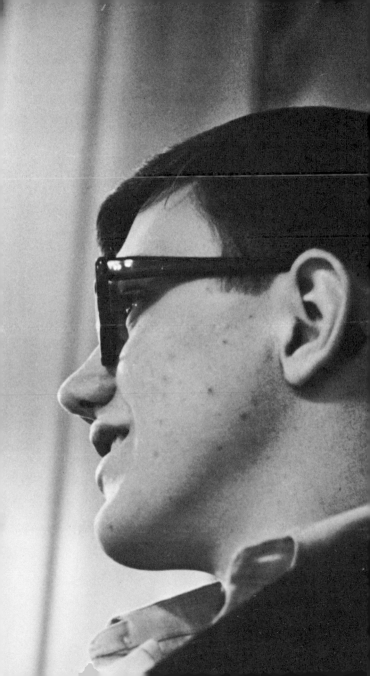

A person must respond
to the honor of being
himself.
This is responsibility:
a response
to our identity
To the deepest
truest
voice in our hearts.

The movie
TO SIR, WITH LOVE
spoke this.
Sir said,
"You are
men.
You are
women.
Act like it
or be satisfied
with being children."
He did not say,
"Do this.
Avoid that.
Jump.
Sit.
Stand.
Walk."
He said,
"You Are."

For the first time they understood they were
people
with honor,
with dignity
deserving respect
IF
they responded to being
men and women.
This dictated their conduct.
Not a law
or policeman
or fear
or "What can I get away with?"
but
PRIDE
in being **them.**

This is a
liberating exciting
moment
of life, to stand eye to
eye with the
world / all that
is beautiful / and
ugly / good /
and evil / and
say Here
I Am!

Every person Must decide himself.
It's simple to substitute obedience to a
law
for living Faith.
This is the greatest dodge of all time.
"Don't do it; you might get caught."
"Is it wrong?"
"Who cares? No one will know."
"The teacher isn't here; go ahead."
"I don't believe in it."
"So what! We can get away with it."
Children at play —
no response
no freedom
terrified
at the great responsibility to BE a Person.
Some people grow old
but never grow up.
Some people grow up
long before they grow old.
We can have Plastic Jesus
by dead obedience to laws.
No faith,
no freedom,
no response
is necessary at all.
The Living God
is somewhere else.

To believe,
(to live
as a child of God)
that I have
dignity
honor
great worth,
is the start of freedom.
Because
I AM ME
many things
actions
attitudes
are unworthy of me.
Not because
a law said
do this
avoid that
jump
sit
stand
walk
but because I am **me.**
Laws may show the way,
illuminate
what is worthy
and unworthy. But,
laws are not ultimate reasons.
What counts is YOUR
code
your faith
your freedom
your honor at stake.

Every sin

is a choice,
a decision of yours
not of the church
nor of anyone else.

It is You standing
eyeball to eyeball
with the situation.
Good is done not because
"I have to do it."
"So many people are watching."
but because
I believe in this.
There is no greater
reward.

RESPONSIBILITY:

a response to
voices
urgings
hopes
desires
in our hearts.
Which way freedom?
Humility for one.
A response —
to be sure enough of our own strength,
and courage
that we can be kind.
(We don't have to crush
bully
destroy
gossip
to prove how big we are.)
Humble enough to say
"I don't know."
Brave enough to say
"I am afraid."
Strong enough to say
"It is beautiful."
Big enough to say
"I don't agree but you are free to speak."

Another voice
deep in the heart
calls for other-centeredness.
Life is dislocated —
nothing fits —
out of joint
till we discover: that what is **really** important
exists
between things —
between me and the world which
lives
and moves
and has its being
in the Living God;
that other people's misery,
their pain,
their happiness,
their joy,
must MEAN something to Me.
When the only REALLY important
thing
in the world is me —
the world is too small to live in.

Perhaps
the
deepest
voice,
the
greatest
need,
is
love.
"What
the
world
needs
now."
Nothing
is
more
difficult
or
necessary.

Love:
creator of real things.
Selfishness:
creator of isolation.
No one can decide for you.
Which?
Choose!
Who are you?
It is your choice.
To use
or serve
to reverence
or play with
to respect
or drag down.
("What can I get away with?")

It is your choice.
Your choice to take the real world
bristling with
pain
loneliness
frustration
weak people
stupidity,
as well as
joy
fulfillment
serenity
giant people
vision.

Your choice to face reality
with its
ups and downs,
or slide off into a dream world.
("...they lived happily ever after")
A terrible temptation to quit the fight:
"I'm not understood."
"The world is phoney; I want out."
"What's the difference? Every one else is doing it."
It doesn't work.
it is YOU —
no one else —
standing in the middle of the world.
"I accept reality.
I will leave it better
than I found it."

Often combining
BEING Christian
and acting Christian
in our own situation —
school
home
classroom
bus
cafeteria —
is not glamorous
fun
easy.
No one waves pennants to
recognize the martyr.
But it is genuine;
it is real.
The phoney does things
he doesn't believe in.
"I'll get caught if I don't".
Follows laws instead of living them.
"I can get away with it. — Why not?"

The world desperately needs action
needs people
but not
JUST
action
and not
JUST
people.

It needs action accomplished by
people
BURNING with Soul,
with spirit.
People who can see
and hear
and feel
and care.

people with
VISION

To build a house is
half
the job.
People must make it a
home.
A community, whether
church
school
team
must be more than people herded together;
it must be a common-unity,
bonded together by a tangible
SPIRIT,
a common
FAITH.
There is all the difference in the world
between one who teaches
and a teacher,
one who plays an instrument
and a musician,
one who goes to church
and a believer.
It is your choice.

The great **beautiful** obligation of YOUTH:
To bring life pulsing with
enthusiasm, abounding in
courage, tempered with
feeling,
to an all too mechanical world.
YOUTH must destroy
Plastic Jesus.

Be satisfied with
nothing less than
the Word / Who
came that we "may
have life + have
it more abundantly

No one can do it
            for you
No one can do it
            but you.

5 THINK ABOU

Who can
separate his faith
from his actions,
or his beliefs
from his occupations?
Who can
spread his hours
before him,
saying,
"This for God
and this for myself;
this for my soul,
and this for my body..."?
Your daily life
is your temple
and your religion.
Whenever
you enter into it
take with you
your all.
Take the plow
and the forge
and the mallet
and the lute,
the things
you have fashioned
in necessity
or for delight...
And take with you
all men:
For in adoration
you cannot
fly higher
than their hopes
nor humble yourself
lower
than their despair.

(THE PROPHET,
by Kahlil Gibran)

So many things:
Faith
Religion
Responsibility.
Yet, only one thing:
YOU.
You
reading
driving
dancing.
You with your problems
with your aches.
Aches with no names.
Sometimes from too much joy
Sometimes too much fear,
All of it —
YOU.
"Who can separate his
faith
from his actions,
his belief
from his occupations..."
God is not on another planet.
Religion is not just
"things you do"·
it is seeing God as a
Person
BECOMING **one** with that
GOD.

look
into the
mirror...
the mirror of
your own
heart

Forget excuses.
Don't run and hide.
Just stand,
LOOK.
Is God a Plastic Jesus?
Are you satisfied with him?
The price is high —
Are you willing to meet the challenge?
Not doing things — but becoming a someone.

Actions are important —
it **does** matter what you
do,
but actions are fruit
growing
on the tree of life.
If the fruit is sick,
you must strengthen the tree,
Cursing the fruit is ignorant.
Jesus
was never fooled by an empty show of
kindness
generosity
charity
the phoney smile
when it was not from the heart.
The "good" people said
"If He knew what
KIND of a woman she
IS
He surely would not let her
Touch Him."
Jesus knew.
She was a person
in need
sorrowing
loving.
She was a lady
daughter of God
Temple of the Spirit.
She returned to her
Father's house.
The tree had become healthy,
the actions flowering from this re-created tree,
beautiful.

Jesus said:
"The Pharisee went to the temple.
Sacks of gold.
Craving attention,
he put on a good show.

the money hit the collection basket.
the people's eyes bulged out.
'See how much he gives.'
'He's got it made with God,'
'How holy he is.'

Far in the back — a widow.
Two pennies.
Quietly,
no one sees.
'Take my heart with the coins.'
Jesus
saw what they did.
More important
He saw what they WERE."
Do you want me to tell you
Which one
the Father loves?
Look into the mirror.
Any hint of
"How Far Can I Go?"
is unworthy
of you
of God
of your relationship to each other.
Pharisee:
"How far can I go?"
Widow:
"Because I love you."
Do you want me to tell you
Which one
the Father loves?

A wife is no wife who says
"How much can I neglect my husband
before he gets angry?"
A mother is not a mother who says
"How many mediocre meals can I prepare
before my family loses respect for me?"
A friend is no friend who says
"How many times can I stand her up
before she calls it all off?"
A good cheerleader never says
"I can't do this cartwheel,
but so what! . . ."
She practices
works
struggles,
till she can.
A real football player never figures
"I'll just fall down;
that guy is too big to tackle.
He dives right in,
digging
grabbing —
maybe breaking his nose.
It doesn't matter;
the tackle HAS to be made.

Even
when it comes to **things**
"How far can I go?"
is unworthy.
A bug on mechanics never thinks,
"What's the cheapest
easiest
fastest
way to hop up this car?"
The important thing is
"How do I make it the best?"

then there is God

"How far can I go?"
"How much can I cheat?"
"How little respect can I get away with?"
"How deaf can I be to your challenge
before the mechanism of our
friendship
trust
communication
blows up?"
A mother
wife
friend
cheerleader
football player
mechanic
is not real with this attitude.
Neither is God.

respect

It starts with
respect.
For yourself
first of all.
Just because you are a
Person
a human being.
This was true of mankind
before the Word
was spoken
by God
to the City of Man.
How much more since we were given the Sign,
Sacrament
Communication
of Jesus Christ!

Mankind given Divinity,
God's own children
sharing His Life,
carrying His name.
Not just for now,
for the journey of earth,
but forever!
"How far can I go before . . . ?"
Unworthy.
The fact of God-With-Us
A reality.
All men.
Community
family
brothers.

"Father, that they all may be
ONE."
All people are
mysterious
deep,
brothers
by just being human.
We are much alike.
Same
fears
doubts
troubles
worries.
Same
ambitions
joys
hunger to be loved and accepted
hunger to laugh and be
With someONE.
All
Called by the Word
to God's family
God's life.
His brothers
and ours.

The Word has spoken the
Challenge
to Be.
Look into the mirror —
what is the response?
yours is a great privilege,
also
a great obligation:
BECOME someONE.
Reject
Refuse to
respond —
this is Sin,
not being YOU.
The Church
does not make you sin;
priests,
nuns
parents
do not make you sin.
Sin is from the inside,
refusing to respect ME,
my brother
God.

In the mirror —

charity

Not just a fancy word,
but an everyday word

made of
smiles
and tears,
anger
and frustration.
Charity —
opposite of

WALLS

"I don't care."
"I don't see."
"I don't have time."
"Look at him — he doesn't fit with us."
"She dresses funny."
"They talk different."
"They are weird."

Walls around us.
(We are safe in here).
Walls around them.
(Thank God they can't get in).
I am an island.
Who needs friends,
someone to talk to
someone to listen
someone to care?

They do.
We do.

How many cruel words spoken,
sharper than any knife.

("Yeah, but they deserve it.")
Let him without sin cast the first word.
("But I just didn't see ... ")
"When did we see you hungry
or thirsty
or naked
or in jail?"
"What you do to your brothers
you do to Me."
("I'm **sorry** but I just didn't see.
It's so hard to see those
next to me,
to really **see** them.")

"But you are the salt of the earth
the light on a mountain top.
My friends,
if YOU do not respond,
hear My challenge,
To whom shall I go?"

In the mirror — "Where's the booze?"
"How far can I go?"
Your response,
your responsibility.
There is no machine
green: go man go
amber: caution
red: you're bombed.

Not a matter of
one
two
three
how many are too many?
Maybe none is just right.
You
must be your own cork.
Does it matter if
respect is lost,
people are hurt,
property damaged.
Does it matter?
"How far can I go?"
No —
"Who am I?"
"A good tree bears good fruit."

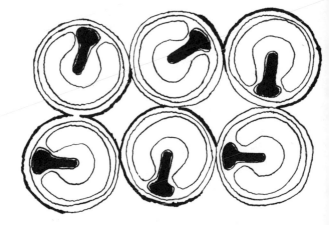

In the mirror — Sex.
The responsibility is too heavy.
Rules!
"Give me rules to follow."
The greatest rule
the most important
the most difficult
the source of all others —
YOU MUST LOVE!
Yourself
others.
Both in God.

Have I really respected
loved
reverenced?

Love is not selfish
does not use others
does not boast
thinks of the one loved before all else.
Love is gentle — but strong
blooms — and has thorns,
is faithful
is faithful
is faithful.
Morality is not just a stopwatch.
(How long can we kiss before it's a mortal sin)
Not only a list of things —
(Let me check the book here
and see if I sinned or not.)

It is **Faith** responding to the code of Christ,
shouting
I Am
ME.

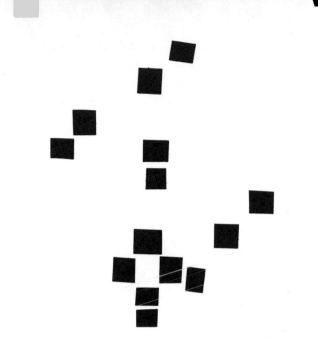

Blue worked on a construction gang
giant man
tough
hands like bricks.
Every Sunday Blue wheeled his wife to Church.
Her mind was ill.
eyes blank
tongue silent.
Maybe she didn't even know Blue was there.

On the job Blue's crew decided to "fix him up".
"Your wife's sick —
he got lots of friends."
"Come on, they'll give you some thrills."
"Who'll know?"
"reasonable."
Blue's eyes filled with pain
disgust
hatred.
"She's my wife.
I love her."
He could not betray
his manhood
her womanhood
their love
God's challenge
to Be.

Sin
Can not come from loving too much
too strongly
too deeply.

love will not hurt... use... abuse the ONE Loved

In the mirror — Things Unseen.
We are light.
How many have we left dark?
We are salt.
How many have we left isolated?
How many have needed a smile
a kind word
a little understanding
a reason to keep going
and gone away empty?
How often has Life knocked at our door
to find us
not home?
God walks on a bridge.
We are that bridge
that sign
that sacrament
that word.
We
are where it is.

A teen age girl wrote a poem:

NOW

Again today — an ordinary day
I see many
Poor
Blind
Uneducated
Crippled
Homeless
Unloved
All of them — the different ones.

Last week — in an ordinary place
I listened to a man tell of these people,
Hurt and suffering
Again and again.
I heard a little girl say she needed clothes
But didn't have them.
And I saw — for the first time —
A man walking across
cold, wet cement, without shoes,
Beaten and bloody.
SAD.
But saddest are the really blind
Who do not understand, yet still judge,
Who refer to little girls as "they,"
Who would not stop to help a bleeding man —
All who could ease the pain.
Some do
Care, give, love.
The man who last week
Talked to me, showed me
I could help another brother
Beaten and bloody.
There are others
Who love
Who follow
One
Who gave himself completely.
Continues to give perfectly
For each
For all.
He is Love, He said.
"As I have done for you,
so must you do in turn."

Bev

156

and the
world
needs
your light
to
shine
through it